OMG! My First Real Job

Tips for the Real Work World

Bronagh Hanley

Somebody had to do it and I figured it had better be me. This guide has been in my head for a long time and is finally on paper. I wish I had something like this when I first hit the workforce, so I hope it is helpful for you. Lots of folks gave me input and advice that made its way into the guide, so thanks to all of you. Special thanks to Ann Dinwiddie Madden for letting me drive her crazy over the cover design; props to the Syracuse University students who shared their stories; love to Patricia France for making me look good; a shout-out to Patti Gunn for her copywriting expertise; and a big smooch to Betty Behrens, who is always looking out for me. And finally, thanks to anyone who is actually reading this. It means a lot.

—BH

Contents:

- Why OMG?   1
- Chapter One: Landing the Job   3
- Chapter Two: The Job Req   10
- Chapter Three: Business Gear   15
- Chapter Four: You Had Me at Hello   20
- Chapter Five: Something to Talk About   25
- Chapter Six: You've Got Mail   33
- Chapter Seven: Eating In and Out   41
- Chapter Eight: Cubeville   48
- Chapter Nine: The Big Bad Boss   53
- Chapter Ten: Off the Clock   59
- Chapter Eleven: Phoning It In   63
- Chapter Twelve: The Meeting   68
- Chapter Thirteen: Your Online Life   76
- Chapter Fourteen: Work Peeps   82
- Chapter Fifteen: The Money Pit   90
- Chapter Sixteen: Off-Sites   97
- Was It Worth It?   102

Why *OMG*?

Everyone knows that the transition from school to work isn't always smooth and can be anticlimactic. It sounds glamorous to be working at Google or *Vanity Fair*, right? There will be some cool projects and good times, but there is still all the other work in between. Working your butt off and not making tons of money can get you down. But you have to start somewhere, because you're only going to keep moving up.

This guide offers realistic and practical advice for recent college grads just starting out. From what to wear to work and how to talk to your boss, *OMG* offers a list of tips to keep you on your toes in every type of work situation.

Let's face it: If your table manners are bad, you're constantly late for meetings or you're overly familiar with the boss, you aren't scoring points. The little things sometimes add up and turn into a big thing, and by then it's too late. You don't have to change who you are. You can still be you and get the job done, right? Don't think you have to compromise

1

yourself to fit in at a company. You don't. But there are some basics that will get you in the right groove.

When you are in that groove, you can contribute to the success of your company instead of working against it. The reason that businesses are so successful is the mix of people who work there. Think about it. If a company had everyone with the same personality and skill set, they wouldn't be able to innovate or be competitive. And businesses want to be functional and profitable. Really. They may not be those things when you are working there, but that is their end goal—even nonprofits.

So remember, the world is a small place and you never know when the same folks you worked with at your first job will be the head of your dream company down the line. The best strategy is to work hard, be yourself and give it all you've got. If you are smart, loyal and creative, you will succeed.

Chapter One: Landing the Job

Nobody wants to hear about your parents' divorce or how your cat died when you were 12. And under no circumstances should you bring anyone other than yourself to an interview. Not even your mom (yes, this actually happened). Do your research, learn the names and titles of the interviewers, have a prepared answer for why you are right for the job and listen to what they are saying. It works, it really does.

The Search: The best place to start is with friends and family; send out an email asking if they know of any entry-level positions that are in your field of interest. Then search sites that you frequent and see if they link to any job sites for that area of interest. Also check out the majors like Craigslist.org, Monster and Indeed, as most HR folks post online. Also think about your focus; try to marry your passions with your skill set and search for jobs in those industries. If you are going to be working at a job 50 or 60 hours a week, wouldn't it be awesome if it were doing something you loved?

The Resumé: The resumé is a very personal thing. It should reflect your style and sensibility while making clear your job objective, your experience, and your skill set and interests. There has been a lot of discussion lately about including a picture on your resumé, but it isn't necessary, since you should get the interview on merit and not on how you look.

Networking: Make a list of businesspeople you know, then a list of companies you admire, and then search industry groups or organizations that support your field of interest. Come up with a master list of companies to which and contacts to whom you can send a personal email with your custom resumé.

The Pre-Interview: It is so important to research the company, the position you are applying for, the person interviewing you, the competitors in the marketplace and the prospective employer's current projects. With Google at your fingertips, there is no excuse for not being well informed.

The Sales Pitch: Hone your elevator pitch—this is the three-minute story of you—and practice it in front of the mirror before you go on an interview. You need to look like you know what you are talking about. If you can't sell yourself, why should they hire you to sell them?

A Portfolio: For many prospects, it's expected that you bring several examples of your work to an interview to show what you can do. It is common for a number of interviews to be scheduled with several executives in the company over the course of a few hours. One of these people is going to ask you for a work sample, whether it is writing or graphics or whatever that job entails. Bring three or four items that showcase the breadth and scope of your work. The sample can be as simple as an itinerary for a conference you set up or the white paper you researched and presented on the state of that industry. Don't bring in the 4" binder with everything you've ever done in your life; no one has the time or interest to go through it all.

Zen Attitude: People laugh at the power of positive thinking, but it makes a difference. If one person shows up for an interview with a positive and enthusiastic attitude, they are going to get the job over the other person who is not confident and seems disinterested. Listen to what is being said, be aware of the tone in which you deliver your answers and display confidence in yourself; these are the nonverbal cues that help an interviewer decide if you are the best person for the job when they are choosing between two equally qualified candidates.

Don't Be Tardy: If you know you are going to be late (which you should really try not to be), call ahead or email and let them know that you are on your way. They would rather know you're still coming than sit there getting more and more irritated that you haven't shown up. Most people live in the real world and understand that things come up. However, if you are late for the third callback interview, the job will definitely go to someone else.

The Sit-Down: When you are front and center in an interview, make sure you talk about results and outcomes instead of getting mired in the details. Managers already know you can make a phone call or schedule a meeting; they want to know that you understand their business and their goals. Whether you are applying for a job as the secretary or the CFO, you need to show an understanding of the company and what you bring to bear on its success.

Dress for Success: Unless otherwise instructed, wear a suit. You can give it your own style and flair, but it still needs to be business attire. Whatever you wear should also cover up your tats if you have any; it's best to unveil those after you land the gig. Some companies will specifically instruct you to wear business casual or dress down if that's their culture. If you don't have any information on the dress code, don't feel comfortable asking HR or don't have any friends at the company to ask, go with the suit.

Money Talks: When a job is posted, many times the salary range is included or HR will have clued you in prior to the actual interview process. If you still don't have any idea what the job pays by the time the interview process rolls around, a quick chat with HR is in order. You need to know if this position is even in your ballpark before sitting down with executives. Otherwise, it's a waste of your time and theirs. And please don't ask senior execs about the salary for the position, as most often they don't have a clue.

The Benes: Most companies offer a standard benefits package of 401(k) (sometimes matched) and medical and dental (sometimes vision). Some offer additional perks like stock options, bonuses, complimentary trips and incentive packages. It is best to get the scoop from HR since most hiring managers don't know what kind of package has been put together for the position and they end up looking foolish if you catch them off guard.

Your Pals: It's great if you have friends working at the place where you are applying for a job. It says to your prospective employer that you understand their culture and can deliver more of what they are producing. That said, avoid having your friends launch a lobbying campaign to hire you. A good word doesn't hurt, but most hiring managers legally have to follow EEO laws, which means posting the job and conducting interviews. Lastly, make sure your inside buddies are in good standing with the company. It would be awkward to lose out on an interview because the person who referred you is not considered an asset.

Thank You Notes: Yes, it is very old school, but it is still a good idea to send an actual hardcopy thank you note to everyone at the company who interviewed you. It's fine to send a formal email, but most people appreciate a handwritten note dropped off or sent via mail. The subject matter typically includes a thank you for their time, their insight, and a brief statement of your understanding and appreciation of the job. Don't get all flowery and crazy; the note itself speaks volumes about your character and may even be the deciding factor between you and another candidate.

Whom You Know: You may very well have gotten the interview because your dad or his college roommate runs the company or heads up one of the client's businesses. It will not help you to point this out to anyone who influences the hiring process. The person interviewing you knows why you are there and you need to prove yourself on merit. Just like everyone else.

It's always hard to tell if you nailed an interview or not, since most managers won't indicate whether you have the job or not until they make the offer. Once you get the job, you can figure out what works for you and what doesn't.

Chapter Two: The Job Req

Starting a new job can be stressful, but staying on your game will make it a lot easier. Make sure your expectations are realistic, understand the job you are taking on and do a little more digging on the company (and your job) before your first day.

The Job Description: Your job is always going to change and evolve as a company expands or contracts, and you will always have to take on projects that you feel are out of your realm of interest. There are a few things you can do to maximize your growth in a job and manage multiple projects: actively communicate with your boss about stuff; keep your job description updated as new responsibilities are added and your role expands; and add any new skills or accomplishments to your resumé to keep it fresh. That way, when it comes time for a raise or promotion, you have a good case for your bump.

The First Few Days: It's always awkward starting a new job—anyone who says otherwise isn't being honest. You don't know where to go, you have no stuff yet, you get to stress about what to wear and you don't know anyone. Some of your new colleagues will go out of their way to talk to you; others will ignore you until they need you for something; and some others may never take the time to learn your name. Just make sure you are friendly, ask questions and introduce yourself to everyone. Put yourself out there and see what happens.

Taking It All On: There is a fine line between being the group brown-noser and stepping up to take on new projects. When the boss asks you to take on additional work or requests volunteers, ask yourself if this project is a good fit for your skills, is something you can get excited about and if it is something you can actually get done in the time allotted. Don't just say yes all the time to impress—you will get buried.

The Salary: You probably won't know what everyone in your company makes unless you work for the government or spend a lot of time searching sites like glassdoor.com. Salaries can vary greatly within groups and for the same job, depending on work experience, time with the company and skill set. Before making a stink about being underpaid or bragging about your take-home pay, make sure you factor in things like health benefits, stock options, bonuses, etc.

Making a Name for Yourself: If you consider yourself to be really good at or proficient in something that can raise your profile or help the business, say something! Carving out a niche or being the specialist in something makes you invaluable and also gives you access to upper management. Whether it is IT, presentations or sales, let them know that's your thing.

Being a Team Player: Don't be the jerk who throws people under the bus every chance they get. If you feel like you are doing all of the work and making most of the decisions, and then someone else steps in to take the credit, that sucks. Figure out a way to privately set the record straight with your boss and make sure you keep the team posted about your work progress in the future.

The Drudge Work: Nobody likes doing the grunt work. It's boring and endless, but everyone has to do it at some point. Getting coffee, taking notes and running errands are all part of the job. Make it more interesting by buying yourself a coffee on the coffee run, creating a really cool template and dissemination system for the meeting notes, or finding the best and cheapest place for getting invitations printed. You will start to get noticed for taking the initiative and making the most mundane tasks a learning experience.

Speak Up: A lot of people are afraid to offer their opinions when they are new to a company. Other people offer their opinions every bloody time they get a chance. If you have something to say, make sure it is valuable to everyone in the room, is relevant to the discussion at hand and is based in fact. The boss will be more impressed with someone who pipes up when they have something really valuable to say rather than with someone who is always dropping their two cents into every conversation.

Work-Life Balance: The U.S. has one of the longest work weeks in the world, with 45+ hours being the norm. Factor in commute times, travel and work events and you are spending a lot of time on the job. Try to make some time for yourself during the day, whether you go for a walk, do a little shopping online, run to the dry cleaners, hit the gym or meet a friend for coffee. If your work is getting done, no one will bat an eye at your squeezing in some personal time. It is also important to set limits for yourself. There is always work to be done and not enough time to do it, but unless you are working on a serious deadline project, it will be there tomorrow.

Keeping It Real: Sometimes people have an image or ideal of what a vice president is or how a sales director behaves, and then they become that person.

It is a little scary to watch as your friend morphs into this crazy corporate drone. You can be yourself and still be great at your job. You don't have to lose your sense of humor or your funky style. Those things make you all the more interesting and contribute to the diversity of your company.

Minding Your Business: It is so easy to jump into everyone else's business at work. You spend a lot of time in close quarters with these folks and you hear and see a lot of stuff. Just remember this rule of thumb: If you don't want anyone meddling in your business, keep your nose out of theirs. It gets too complicated and creates unnecessary drama.

After figuring out all the other stuff to get ready for work, you then have to figure out what to wear.

Chapter Three: Business Gear

You've seen it. We've all seen it. And most often we've seen too much of it. From baring the cleavage to wearing what amounts to pajamas, guidelines obviously need to be set about work wear. The dress code at most places has changed drastically over the past several years. The casual Friday vibe slowly seeped into the rest of the week and has morphed into what we now call business casual.

Business casual is hard to define, which is why many folks miss the mark. Use common sense to decide what works for you. Look at the company's website, check out blogs from employees and search for any photos online to get a better sense of the company culture. Also think about where you work. If you never, ever interact with anyone at work, maybe it is okay to wear your pajamas, but the boss probably wouldn't be thrilled. Most people interact with a ton of different internal and external folks throughout the day, so it's better to wear something that is more appropriate.

People will judge you on your personal appearance whether you like it or not. So it's worth the time and effort to make yourself presentable.

The Money Shot: No one wants to see it at work. Save it for the club or the bedroom. This applies to both men and women. Ladies, no major cleavage, big hair, bedazzled gear or short-short skirts. Fellas, keep the buttons buttoned, the pants a little loose and the boxers out of sight. It's distracting, unprofessional and makes a statement about your approach and intentions, whether you mean it to or not.

The Surprise Meeting: Whatever you wear to work on any given day should work if you are called into an important meeting at a moment's notice. If you can't quite get it together every day, then it's a good idea to keep a nice jacket and an extra pair of shoes under your desk or in a drawer so you can pull yourself together in minutes. It also doesn't hurt to have a few things in your desk to freshen up: deodorant, lotion, mints and a lint roller are desk staples.

All Legs: In some work environments, shorts are all good. If you work in such a place, remember that you still need to look clean and tidy, so no paint-stained, torn or too-short shorts (and yes, this includes cut-offs). Sometimes the opportunity to flash some leg is irresistible. Do the sit-down check if you aren't sure. If your skirt rides up so far that you can see your panties when you are sitting down, it's too short for work. And shorts on guys in the office are always a miss, unless you are doing some outdoor activity that requires them. You want people to take you seriously and not get distracted by what you are wearing.

On Your Feet: Flip-flops and very casual sandals are everywhere these days. Unless your place of work is near the beach and you are going there later, opt for something a little more sophisticated like cool sneakers or leather boots. Shoes do make an outfit. And they can also ruin it, so keep the raggedy shoes in the closet for walking the dog.

Bling: Wearing your entire jewelry collection to work is not attractive for the ladies. And gold bracelets, chains and pinky rings are too much all at once for the fellas. Less is more. The whole concept of jewelry is to accessorize an outfit, not be the outfit. Keep it classy and sophisticated with one or two key pieces and let those shine.

Pig Pen: It is really important to do a self-check in the mirror before you leave the house. Wearing a sweater covered in cat hair or a stained or torn shirt gives the impression you are a hot mess. Even if you really are a mess, you can fake it on the outside. A lint brush, stain remover and a steamer should be your new best friends.

Nit-Picking: A couple of times a day, it's a good idea to do a nit test. Check your hair for knots, your nose for boogers and your skin for zits. If you don't, consider the amplification of fluorescent light and the fact that most people are sitting down when you first encounter them. You don't want to be the one walking around the office with TP on your shoe or a barrette hanging out of her hair, right? People notice if you are well-groomed and it reflects self-respect. Why do you think manscaping is so popular these days?

Heels: Heels are cute. They are a great way to show off your legs, give yourself a little height and boost your self-confidence. Hooker heels or ones that make you stagger around the hallways are just not right for work. If you can't walk properly, they hurt so much that all you do is complain or they are the only item of your wardrobe drawing notice, don't wear them to work.

Navel Gazing: One would think this is so obvious that it doesn't have to be said. Wrong. Here goes. Otherwise known as the "flesh belt," showing off your midriff at work is out of the question. It's not classy and it's not cute and no one wants to look at it, so cut it out.

Bag It: Carry a bag to work. One bag, that is. Not a brown paper bag and a cloth shopping bag and a purse and a gym bag. Invest in one bag that holds all of your stuff, whether it's your lunch, gym clothes, sneakers, laptop, whatever. Carrying a ton of bags makes you look crazy and disorganized.

Scents: Keep the cologne and perfume to a minimum, please. If your scent lingers in a room, on someone's clothes or on office hardware, you have a problem. Overwhelming people with your favorite spritz makes them want to get away from you as fast as they can and makes them wonder what other smell(s) you are covering up.

Remember to showcase your own style and make a statement. Just keep it clean, neat and relevant to your surroundings. Now, on to introductions.

Chapter Four: You Had Me at Hello

As far as introductions go, the high-five is overrated. Leave it to sports teams and kids on the playground. The introduction sets the tone for the rest of the conversation, so give it a little thought. The woman who gave her new boss a hug after learning that she got the job? It definitely made him question his decision. Think about how to play your hand.

The Handshake: For those of you who are unfamiliar, the handshake is a short ritual in which two people grasp their right or left hands, often accompanied by a brief shaking of the grasped hands. It is commonly done upon greeting, parting, offering congratulations or completing an agreement. It is also commonly used across cultures and is the standard business greeting in the U.S. across genders. If you are traveling in another country, check online to determine the introductory etiquette. Some cultures find the handshake to be too personal for a first meeting and other countries use their hands for things other than shaking, so best to check.

Logistics: When you are meeting someone for the first time, it is most appropriate to first stand up, then extend your right hand for the handshake, and state your name and role in your company. If you have a card, now is an appropriate time to pass it along. One little party note: If you are having a cocktail at a business function, always hold it in your left hand so you don't shake with a cold and clammy wet hand.

Hugs and Kisses: A recent phenomenon in the U.S. workplace is the hug and kiss. It is definitely big in the entertainment industry and is quickly becoming the norm in many businesses. The best way to judge the situation is, if you don't know the person well enough to invite them into your home, a hug and a kiss are inappropriate. It makes many people uncomfortable and creates a sense of familiarity that can be counterproductive in a meeting. If you conduct the hug-and-kiss introduction, make it short and sweet. No lingering 'cause that's icky.

The Hello: People seem to forget that the words they use to communicate define how they are perceived. Greeting people with "Hey" or "What's up?" is usually best for your buddies. A polite "Hello" or "Hi, nice to meet you" is a better option for business. If you know anything about the person or their company, comment on a recent success or promotion, if appropriate. Just make sure you don't outshine your boss or overtly seem like a brown-noser.

Look Me in the Eye: It's amazing how many people in the business world don't make eye contact. Stop and think about it for a minute. If you are in a business environment and you are either meeting someone for the first time or managing a project with them and you can't look them directly in the eye, the impression they get is that of a lack of confidence or disinterest on your part. Looking people in the eye shows that you are interested and engaged, but don't do the eye lock and hold eye contact for the entire conversation—that's a little creepy. There is a happy medium for everyone. You will know it when you find it.

Proper Names: If you and your colleagues have nicknames for each other, don't use them in a meeting or in front of a client. It makes the situation unprofessional, especially if you are pitching a big money deal or a new business opportunity. Just call people by their given names and leave it at that.

The BS Meter: If you try to hang with the big dogs and talk about a subject you know nothing about, it will be brutally and painfully apparent to all involved in the conversation. Stick with what you know and research the topic at hand so you can actually drop a few smart bombs here and there.

Religion and Politics: Unless you work for a religious or political organization, steer clear of religion and politics. People get very emotional and defensive with regard to their personal beliefs and discussing, debating or dismissing any religious or political view does not make for a light-hearted situation. There are also legal concerns surrounding these two issues that could get you into hot water if you misspeak, so keep it simple and avoid them altogether.

The Totem Pole: When coworkers are introduced in a meeting or at a business function, introductions are made from the most senior folks to the most junior. The most senior will be leading the meeting and it makes sense for them to kick it off after the initial introduction. Make sure everyone in the room has been introduced because you won't want to be the only one sitting there who hasn't been acknowledged.

Faking It: If you are introducing people whose names you don't know or don't remember, a little trick is to introduce them to someone else. Here goes: "This is Suzy from accounting. She handles the processing on your account." Then pray as hard as you can to the name gods that they will state their name to Suzy in return.

People's Titles: Avoid introducing colleagues present in the meeting by their title or job function, as in "Betty, our assistant" or "Gina, the PR girl." It diminishes that person's role and sets the tone for how they will be treated. Everyone is an equal player if they have been invited to the meeting; otherwise, they wouldn't be there. It will become obvious, as it always does as the meeting unfolds, who's running the show.

Once you have met someone, you most likely have to talk to them, so it makes sense to spend a little time on communication.

Chapter Five: Something to Talk About

When you think about how easily information spreads and can be misinterpreted, it is really important to put some thought into what you say, especially if it can affect your personal reputation or the company's image. You really don't want to be the guy who talked about his company's quarterly presentation at a bar and one of those folks listening was an intern at a prominent media outlet who dished the story the next day.

Slang: Please, oh please, use professional language and not slang, and maybe even proper grammar and the correct pronunciation of words. People make snap judgments about your intelligence and capabilities based on your vocabulary and pronunciation. If you don't know the proper word or pronunciation, look it up.

Who's Talking Now? If and when someone is talking in a meeting, wait until they are finished to make your point. Don't interrupt them until there is a lull in the discussion where you can add your two cents. If you aren't finding that opening, make a note of your question or concern and then raise it before the meeting concludes.

Get in There: When you do have your moment to shine during a conversation or meeting, take advantage of it and share relevant anecdotes and stories that relate to the topic at hand. This is your chance to show your stuff; just make sure you don't get overexcited and go on and on about something if you've already made your point.

The End Goal: Everyone has been in a useless meeting where there is no agenda or stated goal and the conversation heads off on a million tangents. Time is money, people, and the point of a meeting is to bring people together to utilize their collaborative strengths to achieve an end goal. Make an agenda, stick to it and, when necessary, be sure to steer the conversation back to business.

Across the Pond and Beyond: Say you are meeting with a Brit, an Aussie or even with a Finn. They are westernized and seemingly very American, so all is well, right? Best bet is to hop online and do a quick search to find out if there are any major cultural differences you should know about. This is even more important if you are dealing with someone from a non-westernized country. Take a few minutes to find out what words mean different things in their culture. Many misunderstandings have arisen from a word as simple as "slag" (look it up).

Background Checks: Research the people you are meeting with, their roles in the organization and their purpose at the meeting. Doing a little background research makes you look more vested in the company and prepared for the meeting or project. But don't dig too deep and drop a full profile on them—that could be perceived as stalking.

The Elevator Pitch: Always have a two- to three-minute backstory about your professional self that communicates what you do, why you do it and who you do it for. People want to know about you, so tell them the best parts in a minute or less. You don't want to look like an idiot by not being able to describe yourself.

Assumptions: Never assume you know the right answer or where someone is going with an idea. Ask questions, be clear about the objectives, share information and make sure you are on the same page. Otherwise, to assume makes an "ass" out of "u" and "me."

KISS: Keep it simple, stupid. This is your daily mantra to keep your story, mission and message simple. Some people feel the need to over-explain or explain again. Think about what you are going to say in terms of bullet points in your head. If you feel the need to go on and on about a subject, write a report and give it to the boss later. Don't waste everyone's time with an hour-long dissertation when the CliffsNotes version will do.

Game Talk: Try to check your company's financials or at the very least annual goals so you are in tune with the executive strategy. If you don't know the specifics, keep it general or tell whomever's asking that you will get back to them. Either scenario is much better than their taking notes based on your best guess and finding out later that you were wrong.

The Touch-Up: Whipping out your lipstick to reapply or brushing your hair while talking to someone is just wrong. If you want to do a mid-day touch-up, excuse yourself and go to the bathroom. This also applies to picking your teeth and biting your nails. People talking to you in a work environment don't need that much information on your personal hygiene regimen.

Incommunicado: If you receive an email, a letter or a message that is work related, take a quick moment to acknowledge receipt and indicate your intended course of action. You don't have to provide the answer right away. Just let them know you've received it by replying, "Thanks, got it. Will get back to you." Then you can take your time to craft a smart response within the time allotted. When people don't get any response, they assume nothing is being done and start to stress or plan to assign it to someone else.

Mr. and Ms.: Most kids today call their parents and friends' parents by their first names. And while formal titles seem very old-fashioned, always address individuals by their last name and a formal title unless told otherwise. You don't want to be the one calling the boss's wife Mary when everyone else calls her Mrs. Boss.

Who Says? Many folks think that it is productive to criticize others' ideas when they throw them out there. That's brainstorming, right? Wrong. Constructive criticism has its place, but always soften the criticism with a positive counterpoint, as well as an alternative or complementary solution. Bashing other people's ideas only serves to point out that you have none of your own.

Cursing: Everyone drops the "f" or "s" bomb on occasion; it's completely normal and understandable. However, peppering your speech with curse words is not funny, edgy or cute—it's offensive to a lot of people and makes you look trashy. Use your words wisely.

TMI: Too much information. People feel free to share their most personal thoughts and activities in the workplace, including such topics as messy divorces, hateful relatives or colleagues' love lives. No one wants to know about your sex life, your drinking habits, your OCD or your family drama. Go tell your mama.

Gossip: Is the root of all office evil. If you don't have something positive to say, don't say anything at all. Even if it is your BFF at work, you never know where their allegiances lie and what they might repeat given the right motivation. It always comes back to bite you.

Medical Issues: If you hurt yourself as a result of your job, then you can tell folks how you are doing or update them on your progress, just don't get into the gory details about your upcoming gall bladder surgery or paint a vivid picture of your child's birth that is indelibly burned into people's brains.

Small Talk: Is a part of doing business. It is important to chat with your colleagues in the lunchroom or at off-sites; you can make new friends and learn about what other people do. Ask questions, find commonalities and share anecdotes. Being interested in others gets you noticed and creates a strong network at work, so when the next opportunity comes up, your name will be in the running.

Being Witty: If you are the witty, snarky or pithy sort, it's probably best to keep it to yourself until you have a certain comfort level with the folks in the room. Many people consider joking around unprofessional and may get the false impression that this is how you approach everything in your life, including business. Once you're certain you are on common ground, let loose with the personality.

Sex: You have all been in a situation where someone tells you something sexual that you wish you never had to hear. Think about it like your grandfather or your mom talking about their sex lives. It's not nice to think about or hear about. Have mercy on others and don't share your sexual business.

Analogies and Metaphors: There is a time and a place for everything. Using stories, references and examples are great ways to engage the audience in a presentation or pitch. Make sure they are relevant and interesting (and not too personal).

Conversation is really tricky for many folks, easy for others and incredibly difficult for some. Be confident, clear, to the point and professional. The same goes for email.

Chapter Six: You've Got Mail

The constancy and immediacy of email has changed how we interact in business. It is the primary means of communication and should be used as such. Sending an email to your boss with a grinning emoticon in all lowercase? Not so much. To that end, there are rules that need to be followed when using email (and social media) as a business tool.

Legalese: Most important and critical, emails (and texts and IMs) sent on work servers can be subpoenaed by a company's legal department for any reason; they are a virtual paper trail in the business world. If you don't want the world to know about it, don't send it on the company's system.

What's in a Smiley Face? Emoticons are probably not appropriate when sending a proposal for review, but it may be completely fine to send your boss a smiley face when he/she gets promoted. It's best to avoid emoticons altogether in business emails, since they can be perceived as childish and unprofessional. And you definitely don't want that!

The Format: Always address the email to the person for whom it is intended and conclude the message with a farewell sign-off. If the email is external, use the proper letter format as if you were going to print it out and stick it in the mail. For internal purposes, you can be slightly more casual by using bullet points and lingo from your line of work. Always, always use sentence case in emails. No one likes the e.e. cummings emailer.

Shorthand: You know what I am talking about, right? LOL, OMG, L8TR and NP are very helpful when you are sending notes to friends or acquaintances via IM, texts or even email. Business is a little different. Some people don't know what they mean and others think they are lazy and unprofessional, so best to skip them.

Spell-Check: It's become increasingly clear that many people have decided to forgo learning how to spell properly because of the all-knowing spell-check. News flash! Spell-check doesn't catch everything and can also change the meaning of a sentence by inserting the wrong word. So do a manual read-through, or if it is something really long, have someone else eyeball it.

Typos: Typos = lazy. And even if you are, you don't want them to know that. An email packed with typos, wrong verb tenses, incorrect grammar and misspellings does not inspire confidence in clients or colleagues. Read your emails, spell check them, then read them again before you send them.

The Sign-Off: There are a great many people who sign their emails with "Love, Shelly"; "XOXO, Susan"; "Bye, Kathy"; "See you soon," etc. For business-related emails, none of these sign-offs are going to make the cut. More appropriate endings to an email or letter are "Best," "Regards," "Sincerely" and "Thank you." This also applies to texting and posting. Lastly, it is not okay to have your BlackBerry auto signature say, "Pardon the typos since this message was sent from my handheld device." You can still proofread on a PDA.

Asides: This is the catch-all term for people's personal quirks, like off-color jokes, esoteric references, major brain dumps and sassy comments. Unless you are friends with the person you are emailing, it is best to leave this stuff out. Having a quote from a TV character as part of your auto signature? Not so much.

IM: Instant messaging is the best way to get an immediate answer or have a fun conversation while doing something else that is boring. It can also help at work so you don't have to keep yelling across the cubes or running down the hall. But don't tell your boss to hang on while you wrap up an IM exchange, especially if they can see your screen.

Twitter Happy: If you are constantly tweeting and retweeting things your friends send or things you find while surfing the information superhighway, that info is now public information with a time stamp on it. Sooo, your boss and coworkers may think you have a lot of time on your hands, no? Unless you are tweeting for work or clients, try to keep it to a minimum during office hours.

Facebook: Same goes for changing your status or posting numerous messages throughout the day. A few times is okay, but once you cross a certain threshold (say 3X or so a day), that's considered extreme. Unless, of course, you are on vacation and want to make everyone at the office jealous of your beach time. Then post away.

Surfing 411: Everyone shops online and surfs the Web for personal info while at work. The rationale is that folks spend so much time at work that they need to squeeze these things in during the workday. If you really have to do either of these things, unrelated to work, of course, try to find 30 minutes during the day to fit it all in. You are more focused and your boss isn't constantly catching you searching for those perfect shoes.

Lights, Camera, Action: Often overlooked, but critically important, is the need to be crystal clear in your email about whether you want action taken as a result of the email or if it is just an FYI. Otherwise, you will end up with either no response at all or a ton of unsolicited feedback. Better to be clear than to have a ton of know-it-alls giving you advice.

Misfire: When you are crafting an email or IM to colleagues, coworkers or clients, check the recipient list, the subject line, your grammar and spelling, and the content of the email before you hit send. Nobody wants to get a half-written email, especially if it goes to all the wrong people.

Reply to All: Replying to all with either a wildly snarky comment not for public consumption or the simple word "thanks" is entirely unnecessary. Don't reply all unless you are communicating information that is relevant to the entire distribution list.

Recalled: There are still folks who send out an actual email asking to recall their message. This doesn't work, folks. On some systems and servers you can recall the sent message before the recipient opens it, but after that, you are out of luck. Once it is gone, it is gone (unless you have amazing hacking skills). All the more reason to keep it all business.

The Subject Line: The subject line must include a coherent topic or sentence that addresses the email content or it will get deleted. These two business emails seem to be favorites: FW:FW:FW:FW ?? and RE FW URGENT LOW SPAM. Take a second to update the subject line so the recipient knows what the email is about. Otherwise, it isn't going to get read.

The Topic: If the recipient has to search around in the body of the email to find out what the heck you want or are talking about, they will give up and move on to the next thing. Make your first sentence clear and actionable. The rest of the email should answer the basic formula of who, what, when and where. Email is not the place for a dissertation or a major debrief.

Attached: File attachments are the bane of most people's work existence. Most attachments are fine if they are small text files, but when you start sending a media file, that's when it gets tricky. The best way to handle it if you have to send someone big files is to contact them in advance and ask them how they would prefer to receive the files. Some folks don't want big files clogging up their inbox; others don't know how to unzip files and many PDAs freeze when trying to open an email with a big file attachment.

The Email Chain: You know that email chain you got with everyone's email address and the initial instructions from your boss, as well as a comment or two from everyone else who was cc'ed? Don't keep sending it on and on. When email chains get forwarded, there are many times when they include proprietary or inappropriate information. If you really, really need to forward an email chain, read back through it and clean it up so it makes sense. As emails get longer and the thread stretches, the potential for the wrong information to be shared skyrockets.

Out of Office: If you are on vacation and have someone backing you up, note the dates you will be out and the contact info for your backup. Don't write a paragraph about where you are going and what you are doing. No one cares. They are trying to conduct business and don't want to think about your sipping a margarita on the beach while they are stuck in their hellish cube.

Tone Deaf: Just because it's an email doesn't mean you can be a smartass. Make sure your emails are professional, respectful and thoughtful. People get their feelings hurt easily and they aren't always going to call you on it, especially regarding an email exchange. However, they may very well bring it to your boss's attention.

Stylish: There are rules out there for email yelling or email whispering or winking or whatever. You can still have your own style of communicating, but make sure it reflects your approach to business and not your approach to say, getting a date. There is a big difference in perception and results with each approach.

Email is a perfect business tool and is great for sharing information, negotiating deal terms, meeting scheduling and brainstorming. Just make sure to use it wisely and be polite. Speaking of manners, let's talk about eating.

Chapter Seven: Eating In and Out

Eating around colleagues, at work or as part of a business meeting, is tricky. A business dinner or lunch is just that, discussion of business over a meal. Sure, it is more relaxed than at a conference table, but it is still work. Taking food home for your roommates, ordering extra so you can have lunch the next day, asking for a bite of your client's pasta, starting to eat before everyone has their food ... all no-nos.

The Napkin Dilemma: As soon as you are seated, pick your napkin off the table and place it in your lap. Please don't wait until your food arrives and there is that uncomfortable moment when the waiter has to juggle his food deliveries to shimmy your napkin into your lap so your food can be served. If you have to leave the table at any point, your napkin goes on your chair, not on top of your plate and not with you to the bathroom. And don't pile your napkin on your plate when you are done; hang on to it and either set it beside your plate or place it in your chair when you are leaving.

Breaking Bread: When at a business dinner, offer the bread or other shared items to your guests first and then take some yourself. Always keep passing until everyone has been served. Most restaurants serve a hunk of butter with the bread and that needs to get passed as well. And don't take the whole hunk and slather it on your slice; procure a small amount of butter with your knife and smear it onto your bread or side plate. Only then can you marry the two.

The Reach: Reaching across the table to get something while either you or someone else is in mid-conversation can be very distracting. Plus, it's kind of rude. That said, if you need something from across the table, quietly ask the person closest to it if they wouldn't mind passing it down to you.

Elbows Everywhere: When waiting for your meal or in between courses, it never fails that someone will be lounging across the table with their elbows splayed and their sleeves rolled up. You can rest your hands on the table or even fold them if that is more comfortable, but elbows on the table is considered bad manners until after the meal has concluded.

Utensils: The proper way to use utensils is fork in the left hand and knife in the right. You use the knife to cut and then push the food onto the back of your fork.

Then you eat it. If you are at a fancy place and there are tons of different utensils for each course, start on the outside and work your way in toward the plate.

Finger Food: Unless you are in your apartment with your coworker scarfing wings or at an Ethiopian restaurant munching on that spongy bread, you shouldn't eat with your hands. Fast food is the only other real exception, and if that is your company's idea of a business dinner, you need to find a new job.

Kitchen Food: Do not become the guy or gal who gets the reputation for pouncing on the leftovers in the kitchen. Being the first one there, picking over the items like a vulture and then proceeding to stuff your face is just bad form.

Bagel and Donut Days: There is always one awesome person in the office who brings in food for everyone to share. Then there is that annoying person who forgets that the food is for everyone. Take just one and move along. Stockpiling your plate for Armageddon just makes you look like a hoarder. The other option is not eating any of it at all, but if it's 3 p.m. and that donut is still staring at you, then just eat it.

Picking: Stuff gets caught in your teeth when you eat; it just does. It's gross and you can't wait to get it out, but please don't use toothpicks or your fingernails to dig stuff out of your teeth or mouth at the table. Wait until you get to the bathroom or home. Nobody wants to watch you digging in your teeth for a piece of stray food. Really, nobody.

Smoke Break: Everyone has a strong opinion about smoking. Used to be you could smoke in your office and in restaurants. Most people hate it, some love it and others are indifferent. That said, it is best not to try to catch a smoke during a business dinner. It is poor form to leave the table for an extended period of time other than for the bathroom and, whether you think so or not, you reek when you come back.

Food Noises: In some countries, it is the sign of a delicious meal to slurp your food and chew with your mouth open. Well, we live in a culture that values keeping your trap shut while chewing and slurping only by accident. If you manage to talk with your mouth full or slurp in a noodle or two, a mild "excuse me" should be enough to remedy the situation. Do it all the time and you will find yourself eating alone.

The Powder Room: If you have to go, don't tell everyone at the table. Discreetly leave your napkin on your chair and say, "Excuse me," then head off in the direction of the bathroom. Please don't ask everyone at the table where the toilets are because you have never been there before. Be a grown-up; go by yourself and, if necessary, ask for directions from a staff person.

Digital Devices: Unless you are on a death watch or you have a million-dollar deal closing during the dinner, don't answer your phone or check your BlackBerry. Put both on mute and engage yourself in the task at hand. Give your full attention to the discussion at hand and look at this as an opportunity to learn and develop deeper work relationships.

The Bill: If you are hosting the meal (which means you initiated the invite), you should discreetly tell the waiter before dinner you are handling the bill; when the bill arrives you quietly review and pay it. Refrain from commenting on the cost, the tip amount or the service. If you are out with a group of colleagues, the rule of thumb is that the most senior person at the table covers the bill to expense it later.

Doggy Bags: It is generally not a great idea to request and/or take home food in a doggie bag while at a business meal. Order what you want, eat what you can and leave the rest. Don't take food home for your dog or your roommate, especially if your boss is paying.

The Server: Treat the server with respect and value their service and opinion. How you treat folks serving your meal is indicative of how you treat others in your life. And you never know when that waiter might reappear in your life, maybe as your new boss or client down the line.

Your Order: Don't order the most expensive thing on the menu just because the company is paying for it. Everyone is onto this trick and it's bad manners. When the server arrives at the table, be ready with your order. Don't go around the table asking what everyone else is getting or change your order five times. That is annoying. To everyone.

Sharing Food: Stabbing food off someone else's plate or asking to have some of their entrée is inappropriate for business. It is completely fine when out with family and friends since they will stab your hand with their fork or pull their plate way if they don't want you to have some of their food. Because business colleagues can't or won't, it is better to keep your fork to yourself. You know, personal space, germs, allergies, politeness, etc.

Meal Cadence: It is general practice to wait until everyone has their meal served before starting to eat your own. If only a few folks ordered appetizers, wait until they are all served and then you may begin. Digging in before the time is right makes you look like you don't get enough to eat or that you are completely oblivious to everyone else at the table. The same goes for getting up or concluding the dinner. Wait until everyone is finished and everyone's plates have been cleared before wrapping it up.

The Booze: Most business dinners involve wine, beer and liquor, as do many work cocktail parties. If you are the host, it is appropriate to ask if the table would like wine, unless you know for a fact that they don't drink. Then serve your guests first, don't hog the booze and take it easy on the intake. Two to three drinks are the limit; otherwise, you will be the talk of the town the next day.

And no drinking at the office, unless there is a party, especially if you are in a cube.

Chapter Eight: Cubeville

Okay, nobody likes sitting in a cube. Really, nobody. Who wouldn't want to have an office with walls to the ceiling and a door you can close? So think about it this way: When you are talking about your adventures of the night before or if you have a sexy pic of your honey posted on your bulletin board, remember that you are inches away from the person next to you. And they probably don't want to know that much about you at work.

The Décor: Decorate away and make it your individual space, but keep it clean, both physically and professionally. Your workspace should not look like a bomb went off, you can't find a thing and you have a passion for stuffed animals. Be organized, don't get too personal and remember that your space reflects your personality and your role at the company.

Meals on Wheels: Bringing leftovers and eating them at your desk is a great way to save time and money. Bringing stuffed cabbage from the Russian joint in your neighborhood is just wrong. Think about what you are doing to the office atmosphere before firing up the microwave. Your colleagues will appreciate the consideration.

Eavesdropping: Say you are sitting in your cube working away and minding your own business and you hear a coworker ask someone else a question or comment on the news. You know the answer or want to make a comment, so do you just jump in? Do you send them an email? The golden rule of cube living is that unless you are being spoken to directly, you mind your own business. Catch up with that person later, but don't make it a cube free-for-all.

Art Work: Everyone has different tastes and different tolerance levels for what is considered "art." Hey, some people find the naked human form really appealing, while other folks have mad body issues. Some people think collecting key chains is museum-worthy, while others have eschewed material possessions. Whatever your thing, keep it to a minimum in the office. One or two tasteful (in your opinion) pieces around the cube are great. Anything more than that borders on kinda crazy and will have people betting on the numbers of cats/dead bodies/stuffed animals in your apartment.

Personal Calls: Making a few personal calls here and there throughout the day is all good. You need a break, and a few minutes catching up with friends is a great way to re-juice. But keep it short and simple. Please don't recount anything sexual, medical, familial, stressful or disturbing. If you need to get "personal," go somewhere private.

Lurking: Everyone has a cube lurker in their office. They're the ones who are always there when you turn around and seem to have endless amounts of time to chat about inane subjects all day long. Tell them you have work to do and want to use your time wisely, and move on. If you're the lurker, be respectful of people's limited privacy and time.

The Toss: Believe it or not, some people really get into looking through other people's crap. It's weird, yes, but not at all unusual. If you have something you don't want anyone to see, don't leave it in your cube. Whether they are in the office working late after hours and need a bite or are just bored, these folks have been known to dig deep for no reason.

The Unwritten Quiet Rule: Sometimes people have to write a report, make sales calls or just get their work done, and it is perfectly reasonable for them to invoke the quiet rule. This means that everyone in the surrounding cubes has to shut up for a set period of time so that person can focus. Don't be the one who constantly breaks this rule while invoking it when you need the quiet time.

Printerdom: It is a tricky thing sharing a printer with a group of people. You have to print out the directions to the show tonight or the invitation you got for the party this weekend, but you don't want to be the one who jammed/locked/queued up the printer with personal crap so everyone else can't get their work done, do you? Best to print quickly and stealthily at lunch or right at the end of the day when you can hit print and snatch that puppy before anyone else even notices.

Crown Jewels: Even in the nicest offices, there is going to be a thief. Leaving your wallet, purse, briefcase, watch, iPod, PDA or any valuable personal stuff in your cube is a bad idea. This goes for papers too—your insurance cards, Social Security information, no matter what—someone can lift it and you wouldn't even know. Lock it in a drawer or take it with you when you go.

Guests: Who doesn't like a visitor during the day? Set up an extra seat in your cube so someone can take a load off and shoot the breeze with you for a few. Even have a few laughs. Just keep in mind that your colleagues are inches away and they are part of the conversation too, whether they want to be or not.

Cubes are here to stay, so we'd better get used to them. And it's hard to complain when your boss is also sitting in a cube. Speaking of bosses …

Chapter Nine: The Big Bad Boss

Your mom may be your best friend and tell you you're special, but don't think your boss is going to do the same. Your boss is not your BFF from the get-go. They may be nice to you, and mentor you, and take you out to lunch, but don't make the mistake of treating them like a peer. You are there to learn from them and possibly take over their job one day.

The Approach: Don't always go to the boss with problems. Bring them the problem, along with a couple of solutions, so they can see that you have put some thought into the situation and are offering to take action to resolve it. You don't want to become the one who is always pointing out problems but doing nothing to fix them; that's called complaining.

Taking Their Time: If you have a pitch to make, an issue to discuss or just want the boss's opinion on something, think it through before you take any of their time. You may even want to do a mental run-through of the conversation so you sound confident and, more importantly, make sense. It is obvious when someone has prepared for a conversation, and this preparation will be remembered and respected.

Back Talk: It is amazing how many times you hear a subordinate challenge a boss's opinion, answer or statement. It is also really embarrassing. Best to wait until you two are alone and then voice your opinion.

Private Info: When working for someone else, you will likely be privy to personal information about them, their families or their lifestyles. The unwritten and longstanding rule is that this information is off limits, even if you can't stand your boss with all of your heart and soul. You have been entrusted with information that is not yours to share.

Back Stabbing: Everyone makes jokes about others in the office, and this may even include your boss, but don't fall into the trap of badmouthing your boss to people in the office on a regular basis. You will quickly discover that there are very few folks willing to actually say what they really feel in front of the boss and you could be the only one left standing.

Friendship: Some people have managed to be friends with their bosses for years and it works for everyone. It is common that a friendship will blossom after you have left a job and that person continues to serve as your mentor. In the meantime, be respectful, feel out boundaries and remember that you are in a business environment.

Taking the Heat: Sometimes mistakes are made in the workplace and someone needs to save face. Most often, face-saving is reserved for the boss and someone else gets to be the fall guy. Take the heat, but make sure your boss knows that you know the real deal with a private conversation about the actual sequence of events.

Recognition: In most offices, recognition is not offered for accomplishments that are considered within the job description. Unless you have moved mountains and sealed an unusual deal, it is unlikely you will be singled out and recognized by the boss. Results are expected and that is why you get paid.

Leaving the Fold: When you have decided it is time to move on and leave a company, do so in a professional and composed manner by going to your direct supervisor and having a frank discussion. Your immediate boss is the one who will be most affected and will be tasked with replacing your position. Going to the Big Kahuna to submit your resignation inflates your sense of importance (unless, of course, you report to that person) and undermines your immediate supervisor, who will remember this forever.

Getting Fired: If you are fortunate or unfortunate enough to get terminated from your company, it is important to keep your head up and leave with grace. This is hard to do when you are being walked out by security in public and you barely had time to throw your personal belongings into a box, but that will be the final impression you leave with everyone and you want it to be classy.

The Personality: If your boss is one of those personalities whom everyone loves and wants to be "in" with, but you know that he or she is really just a blowhard who dumps all the work on you and takes the credit, just keep doing what you need to do to get by. These folks seem to do well in business and no amount of bitching, reporting them to superiors or talking to them will change that. They found their formula and they are sticking with it. You're the one who needs to find a new job or boss.

Boss Tasks: There are certain things you have to put up with as lower management and many bosses have been waiting for their chance to exert their power and control. They may ask you to get their dry cleaning or pick up their cat from the vet or put you into a position where you have to lie to their spouse or cover for them in the office. There is a fine line to walk here, especially if you have a close relationship with your boss. But unless the task is part of your job description or involves learning the business at hand or developing key business skills, I would say, "No thanks."

The Raise: When you go to the boss to ask for more money, make sure you are familiar with the company's current finances, have done your research on comparable salaries in the marketplace and can back up your request with a business rationale. Many companies have a raise scale based on a review process and that determines your raise—no ifs, ands or buts. If your company doesn't work with a review system, you are responsible for making a clear-cut business case for your value add.

Inside Baseball: You will inevitably be stuck in an elevator, at a work function or at a kid's softball game and run into the boss or big boss. Make sure you know the latest news on your company and have some office buzz to share. You are going to have to make small talk and it most likely will be about work, so it's better to have a few talking points in your back pocket.

Making nice with the boss is always smart, but don't compromise your ethics or morals to please someone else. What goes around comes around. The same applies when you are off the clock with colleagues.

Chapter Ten: Off the Clock

Being out of the physical confines of the office with colleagues for a happy hour, pizza party, bowling or whatever doesn't give you permission to let your hair down and get wild. Save that for your friends.

The Meanies: There are always going to be people in the office who don't like you. They may be competitive or want your job or have aligned themselves with someone else, or they could be just plain mean. In any case, watch your back, don't give them any ammo and don't let them see you sweat. Especially at happy hour after work.

Don't Clique It: Try to talk to everyone in the room and not just hang with the folks you see every day. Go chat with the receptionist for a moment or the guy from finance that processes your invoices or even some of the top executives. The more people you know, the greater your success when you need to complete a big project, as you can go to them as resources.

Watch Your Tone and Manner: Don't be flirtatious, or conversely, too professional. Be straightforward and personable in your manner and talk about things that are relevant to your business, current pop culture trends or travel. Be yourself (unless you are a total jerk, then you can fake being a nice person).

The Chatter: Talk about subjects that mean something to the business or the person you are talking to, such as recent trends in your field, their hobbies or vacations. Straying into personal territory is uncomfortable for many people and puts them on edge. Current events, trends, anecdotes and stories are always a good bet, but keep it clean.

What Not to Wear: Don't go to the company picnic in your clubbing outfit. If you are going out clubbing afterward, put on the basics (jeans and a shirt) and add everything else when you leave. Trust me, you will be happier that everyone is not checking you out, in a bad way.

Boozing It Up: Pace yourself on the booze front since you are with people who sign the paychecks that make the rent. It is fun to have a few laughs and a few drinks, but you don't want to be the one with the lampshade on your head and the hangover the next morning.

The Hairy Eyeball: Whether you like it or not, some folks in management will be watching you out of the corner of their eye. They want to see how you handle yourself outside of the workplace. Don't stiffen up, but definitely keep yourself in check. The execs may have their eye on you for a new gig or a big project and want to see how you handle yourself in certain situations.

The Host: Make sure to acknowledge and thank the person who put the gathering together. They may be the boss's assistant or the office manager, but they put a lot of work into making sure you and your colleagues had a good time, and that should be noted. It's guaranteed that you will be one of a handful of folks who actually said thank you.

Bring Something: It is appropriate to show the same graciousness at a work get-together as you would in someone's home. Whether it is a bottle of wine, a game or a handmade token, people remember small gestures. And it's good manners.

The Wallflower: Don't be the goof standing on the sidelines snickering and gesturing with your equally judgy colleague at a work event. This may be fun for you, but everyone else will think you are a snarky snob and not a team player.

Funny Business: If you have ever watched an old (read sexist) movie or even old TV series, you will note that office parties were a chance for folks to get crazy. It is funny to watch on screen, but absolutely horrifying to watch in person. Plus, everyone remembers bad behavior and talks about it for ages. Steer clear of the party PDA.

Last Call: There is no need to stay until the bitter end of the party. Unless it is a sit-down dinner and show, in which case you are obligated to stay for the duration, it is polite to stay for about an hour and a half. Then make sure to say your goodbyes to the key party people, your boss and the host before really kicking up your heels elsewhere.

Hanging out with your colleagues outside of work can be a good time. Just remember to keep it simple and read the room. What is definitely harder to gauge are phone manners, what's right and what's wrong. Listen up.

Chapter Eleven: Phoning It In

"Yeah." "I got it." "What's up?" "Hey." These have all become commonplace intros when answering a phone. And no, these were not the answers to personal phone calls. Giving good business phone is a must.

Get to the Point: We have all heard them, the rambling messages with the ums and the ahs thrown in for good measure. A message is just that: state your business after a cordial hello and call it a day. The same goes for calling someone with an idea or a proposition. Most people are too busy to talk for an hour and will start to avoid your calls in the future if that is your M.O.

Who Are You? How are you supposed to call someone back if they don't leave their number? Or if they speed-talk through the whole message and you still don't get any info after replaying it five times? Leave your name, number, email and order of business, and then repeat your name and number at the end. Keep it short and sweet. Also, if you have an unusual name, make sure you spell it or phonetically pronounce it, which makes it easier for everyone.

Conference Callers: If you are the one to set it up and book the phone bridge, then be the one to test it before the meeting to make sure it works. Also double-check the numbers you send out to everyone to make sure there are no transposed numbers or incorrect area codes. This makes it so much easier than having to manage that flurry of emails and calls at 10:02 when everyone is scrambling to make the meeting and can't connect.

The Speakerphone: This old-school gadget serves a purpose and that is to ensure that everyone can hear what the folks on the other lines are saying. Never put someone on speakerphone without their knowledge or consent. It can be potentially embarrassing and deal-breaking. And don't assume the mute button is idiot-proof. It isn't.

Response Time: If someone leaves you a business message on your voicemail and you don't respond to them because you haven't started that project, you don't know the answer or it isn't at the top of your priority list, just get back to them and let them know you are on it. Shoot them an email or leave them a quick message. It makes everyone feel better and you just got some props.

Ringtones: Lil' Wayne may be your favorite artist in the whole wide world, but that doesn't mean it should be the ringtone on your phone. When your phone rings in a meeting and everyone gets to listen to your musical tastes, it doesn't make you look hip and cool—just unprofessional. If you really feel the need to get your groove on your phone, turn off the ringer before you head into a business meeting or get together with clients.

Vocal Volume: When you are talking on the phone to family, a friend or an associate, there is absolutely no need for you to be speaking in your "outside" voice. If you have a bad connection or the person can't hear you, step outside or check the volume, but leave the meeting or situation so everyone else doesn't have to stop talking and listen to your yelling.

Holding: Hold music has gotten so much better than the soft rock madness that used to be the norm. That said, if you do put someone on hold, don't leave them hanging for more than one and a half minutes. Any longer than that and they deserve a callback.

Cell Phone No-No: Unless it is your mother and she has been hit by a bus, don't answer the phone when you are in a conversation with a colleague, getting ready to pay for your latte or are in the process of paying a vendor for their services. It is rude to the person you are interacting with and you can return that all-important call once your business is completed.

Transferring: Note to self: Whenever using a new phone system, figure out how to use all of the important features before testing them when the head of the company calls your line. When you transfer someone to the wrong extension or drop their call entirely, it reflects poorly on the company and makes you look incompetent. Read the instructions or ask someone to show you.

The Answer: When you answer your phone or the main company line, you should say your name or the business name. Please don't answer with "Yes?" or "How can I help you?" People like to know with whom they are talking and it gives them a second to collect their thoughts.

Phone Stalking: Some people think that calling a number repeatedly is the best way to get through to them. What these folks don't seem to realize is that everyone has caller ID now. Even your grandmother. So calling repeatedly to get someone's attention doesn't work. Try once, leave a message and they will get back to you on their own time.

Call Waiting: Multitasking has its own challenges. Handling two phone calls at once is a recipe for disaster. If you can figure out how to toggle back and forth between the two calls without cutting someone off, more power to you. The greater challenge is trying to keep two conversations straight in your head while trying not to be rude to either party. Best to handle just one call at a time.

Timing: Since we are all connected and available 24/7, we can reach out to anyone at any time, right? Wrong. Don't call a colleague's or boss's cell phone outside of business hours unless requested or it's an emergency. Calling from the bar at 3 a.m. to leave a message that you will be late for work the next morning doesn't cut it either. Use email in the off hours and a follow-up call if necessary.

At work, the phone is another tool for you to get your work done, do it well and make a good impression. Just like a meeting.

Chapter Twelve: The Meeting

Being late, chewing gum, interrupting and texting are all cool in a meeting, right? Wrong. Meetings can be a great way to brainstorm, problem-solve and present new ideas. When abused, meetings are a disaster.

The History: Meetings used to involve booze and smokes and take place at all hours of the day. You had to get dressed up and you spoke only when spoken to. Meetings today take place in person, over Skype, on the phone, via text and in video conferences. The same rules apply for all meetings, no matter the format.

Meeting Addicts: There seem to be some people who are addicted to meetings. Something you can talk about in ten minutes in person? Noooo, let's get together a group of 10 people and set up a phone bridge and everyone can chime in. Use your time and other people's time wisely. If a quick chat will resolve the issue, then do it. If it does require a meeting, schedule a reasonable length of time and time of day and invite decision-makers to the table so stuff can get done.

Decisions by Committee: Sometimes it is helpful to have a lot of people weigh in on an issue or come up with ideas. But many times it becomes an onerous and unnecessary process to have more than two or three people involved in decision-making. If you are constantly striving for consensus, you are going to lose sight of your goal and take up a lot of people's time.

Setting the Agenda: It is amazing how many meetings are called with no agenda and no direction. Everyone arrives late and then sits around checking their PDAs until someone kicks it off. Having an agenda keeps everyone on target and on message. If you are running the meeting, have one and distribute it before everyone gets there so they can review it. If you are attending a meeting, ask for an agenda so you can prepare to contribute.

Follow the Leader: Some folks are born leaders and others, followers. Sound familiar? When it comes to meetings, if you called it, you need to be the leader. Even if you are a follower. Understood? Thank the group for coming, introduce the topic, direct the discussion and distribute the notes—all in a reasonable amount of time.

Pay Attention: Giving a presentation in a meeting is a big deal for the person talking. This means that whether you are interested in the topic or not, it is not good form to check your PDA, pull out your laptop or even flip through the distributed deck. Look interested, take notes and give the person your full attention. You would want the same if it were your turn in the hot seat, right?

Participation: There is an adage that states: "If you have nothing good to say, then say nothing at all." This is a good rule to follow. If you are paying attention and the meeting relates to the industry or business you are in, chances are you have something smart to say about the topic. Otherwise, just listen and learn something new.

Discussions: It is amazing how often it happens, but it happens a lot. The guy who hasn't been paying attention but decides he needs to add something to the discussion which ends up being totally irrelevant and dated. The gal who wants to try to talk about something she knows nothing about. Or the boss who starts talking about something totally unrelated to the subject matter being discussed. Follow the discussion, stay on topic, and table your comments or critiques until the end or until you can do your research. Then call a smaller meeting to get the actual work done!

Intros: If you have a roomful of folks who are going to be collaborating on a project, take a few moments to have each person introduce themselves and what they do. Many times, name and role is the best intro for everyone, including those folks taking notes or serving food.

Pitching In: If you get to the meeting early, see what you can do to help set it up. The person may be having difficulties and will appreciate the help. This also applies to after a meeting. If the person is loading up their gear, offer to lend a hand and possibly chat further about the meeting topic. It is good karma and you may learn something.

Constructive Criticism: When providing feedback, always start with the positive. If you kick off with the negative, the person goes on the defensive and all they hear is the teacher from Charlie Brown. Provide positive commentary with any constructive comments. It will be appreciated. And if you are on the receiving end, always thank people for providing feedback, even if you don't like what they had to say.

Invitations: Unbelievable as it may sound, sometimes invitations to meetings are as complicated as a state dinner with a deposed dictator at the White House. The politics abound. If you work in a very political office, it is best to seek guidance from your supervisor to determine the proper invite list and seating for your meeting. If you don't, someone will make you unhappy, and most likely it'll be the one who put the meeting together!

Waiting: Some companies have a running joke that they work on [company name here]-time. Meaning all meetings start at least 10–15 minutes late. This is kind of like saying: "I totally don't mind wasting your time. I had something more important to do." Unless the boss calls from the car to say he is running late and the meeting can't go on without him, start the meeting on time. The latecomers will have to play catch-up and will soon realize that you use your time and their time efficiently and that your meetings are valuable.

The Presentation: Public speaking is a course in high school and college for a reason. It is hard and requires practice. Some folks are naturals (but probably still practice) and others are a disaster. Make sure you always make eye contact, use slides and index cards for notes, keep the copy on your slides to a minimum and focus on visuals, and keep it short and sweet so the group can ask questions and participate. Plus, you can always gain confidence from imagining everyone in the room naked. Really.

Read the Room: Pay attention to your audience while you are talking to see if you are a hit or a flop. If you are bombing, you can still change course and get the crowd on your side. If you are a hit, keep the good times coming. Figuring out where you are midstream and altering your course to meet the needs of your audience will be an important skill to have in both your business and personal lives.

The Munchies: Everyone is time-crunched these days and that has given rise to the meeting with food. Which means that it either sits in the middle of the table and no one eats it but everyone stares at it longingly, or the entire focus is on the food and the meeting degenerates into side conversations. The best way to resolve this issue is to serve food on a side table and ask everyone to grab something before they take their place at the meeting table. They can take what they need and the focus can then be on the meeting topic and not on the food.

The Biz Card Shuffle: It is common practice to exchange business cards with new clients or colleagues when meeting for the first time. Some folks do it upfront at the beginning or at the end upon saying goodbye. No matter the right time, it is standard operating procedure, so having to run back to your office to get your business cards makes you look like a little kid who forgot they were at work. Don't forget the cards.

Podcasts-Skypes: Depending on the company, some meetings are very tech-focused and involve some sort of Web or video component. If you are leading the meeting, make sure to test the equipment and the presentation before everyone arrives. You should also have IT on hand to help you out in case there are any problems. This applies to a two-person meeting with your boss or to your annual conference. The only one who looks foolish if it doesn't work is you.

Brainstorming: Everyone is usually game for a brainstorm. Especially if it is on a project that is out of your usual area of expertise. Make sure to invite a diverse group of folks, provide props or graphics to get everyone thinking, and clearly state what you want to achieve with their brains.

The Hierarchy: Whether we like it or not, there is a certain hierarchy in meetings. For example, if you have invited the chairman of your company to attend your presentation, they still get the seat at the head of the table. It doesn't matter that this is your meeting. What matters is that they run the company. Always defer to the most senior person in a meeting and solicit their feedback and comments, even if you know it is going to be painful. It builds character.

Meetings done right can be really creative, constructive experiences that enhance your understanding of a company and let you play a deeper role in the business process. They can also be used as a vehicle to push people's individual agendas or a time for folks to catch up and gossip. You get out of it what you put into it. While we are on the subject of putting it out there …

Chapter Thirteen: Your Online Life

With the wildfire spread of news and gossip online, an individual's personal behavior is more relevant to their company's reputation than ever before. Always remember that your online profile includes a lot of personal information that pops up across a number of different sites, from pictures and geographic location to marital status and number of friends and taste in music. It's cool, right?

What's not cool is when human resources at your dream job Googles you before the interview or your friend gets fired because of pictures you posted of her or when your boss sees that tweet from the ball game the day you called in sick. Everything you post online lives there for all to see, forever.

Public CV: It is commonplace nowadays to have your resumé or CV posted in numerous places online. Make sure that wherever it is, it's updated, results-oriented and makes sense. Including information about your likes and dislikes, as well as other personal info, is a no-go. Just because they live online doesn't make these docs any less valuable for potential employers or recruiters.

Blogging Away: Having a personal blog is a great thing; just make sure it is about something that is important to you. Otherwise, it isn't worth the time or the exposure online. If you are passionate about a subject or know more than anyone else in the universe, then blog away. If you just want to bitch and whine about your company, your friends or some awful tragedy that happened to you, it's probably better to keep a personal diary. What you write online reflects on you as an individual, a professional and a human being.

Wild Postings: Commenting on an online article or about a seminar you attended is right on. You can state your opinion and have your voice heard in an open forum. Commenting just for the sake of saying something or making nasty comments about an article or incident is just plain stupid.

Publicity Machine: Everyone thinks they know how to publicize themselves or their friends. It may not seem like it, but publicity is a strategy that is employed to yield results. If you want to promote yourself, your book or your product, think it through and work toward measurable results. Just sending out an email or making a post about something you think is the next best thing does not make it so.

Photo Evidence: Sharing photos online is a fun and interesting way to interact with your friends, promote an event or product, or generate a discussion about a topic. Who couldn't spend hours on Flickr? But when photos feature you drunk or half-dressed, all that happens is you look like an idiot, forever and for all to see.

Proper Language: Slang has its place in our society and is commonly used in casual conversation and online. When you are presenting yourself as a brand or positioning your company as a valuable resource, stick to proper English. It sets the tone for how the information will be received and it reinforces your message in a positive manner.

Your Pals: The online world breaks down many barriers and increases the dialogue between strangers and friends alike. There's a lot to be said for connecting with folks from your past and seeing what everyone is up to. However, be careful about who you agree to connect with online. Some people are racing to collect as many friends as possible, while others are connected with meaningful folks. Either way, the company you keep speaks volumes about who you are.

Video Resumés: The newest trend on the business scene and a great idea for a number of reasons. Just make sure your target audience is going to be receptive, the content is compelling and interesting, the quality is good enough for a promo piece and the format is compatible with different systems.

Social Networking: Great tool for finding a new job, doing your current job better and connecting with other folks who do what you do. It is helpful to keep some networking for just work and others for just play so your two worlds don't collide and you can be free to be yourself.

Associations and Affiliations: It is a good idea if you are serious about your career to join an association or group either within your company or without. It helps connect you with other people, could introduce you to your mentor and is always helpful for job hunting. That said, if you belong to a club called Geeks for Star Wars, it's probably best to keep that to yourself. There's no need for it to be listed on your resumé or any of your online profiles.

Alumni Connections: Whether or not you had a good time in college, your alma mater is still a great resource for information about classes, connections and developments in lots of areas. Use the online resources that your college tuition paid for and dig into these websites. Post a profile, connect with professors and students, and offer to teach a class.

The Email Address: There are a lot of companies out there these days with funny names that make you giggle and prompt you to check out their website, like shmoop.com. Unless you work for one of these companies, it is best to keep your email address professional and to the point. Using funky names or silly terms in your email address is not amusing to an employer and may prevent you from getting hired. There are a lot of free email services out there. Make the effort and invest in one that gets you noticed for the right reasons.

Passion Play: If you are a closet band geek or a budding thespian ready to hit the boards, use online resources to get in there and make it happen. However, if you are into dog-fighting or acid raves, it may be a better choice to keep that research and those connections private. Whether you like it or not, you are judged on your likes and dislikes, and most people don't approve of the illegal stuff.

Chat Rooms and Forums: Using an online pseudonym is the best way to engage, but a surprising number of folks use their own names. If you want to sound off, do it often and do it well, but use a screen name. You never know who is going to disagree with you.

Using the Web to network and make friends is a great thing, it just needs to be done with some class. The same goes for interacting with your colleagues.

Chapter Fourteen: Work Peeps

Always remember that your work peeps have your back (most of the time). You can count on them for a shoulder to cry on or a sounding board for venting, as well as helping you out in a pinch. Don't antagonize them, undermine them or betray them. They are sometimes all you have. And don't forget about the people who keep the business running behind the scenes: the mail guy, the cleaning folks, the supply person. You mess with them and it's all over.

Be Kind: Sounds like a gimme, huh? Well, it's not. Some people have to be told that the office is not their own little fiefdom and that everyone is not at their beck and call. Treat people with respect and you will get the same in return.

Taking Credit: Don't be a glory hog. Recognize people's contributions and give them credit for their work and ideas. Your moment in the spotlight will come and, until then, you will be recognized for being a team player. Yay.

Personal Space: Different cultures have different rules of engagement when it comes to personal space. Here in the good ole U.S. of A., we like our personal space. A lot. When someone enters this space, it is very uncomfortable and makes it hard to concentrate on anything except how close the person is to you. The golden rule for comfortable interaction is a minimum of 15" of space between two people.

The Attitude: If you are a vice president in your office and one of your colleagues is a manager, but you guys are the same age and have the same educational and socioeconomic background, there is no need to cop an attitude about your position. Come to think of it, this also applies to outside your company too. People who act as if their you-know-what doesn't stink, well, they stink.

Money, Money: Before there were websites that listed what people made and the annual *Parade* magazine issue with the same, the only place you could get salary info was from the GAO for government work. There is a good reason for this. Talking about what you make outside of your immediate family or financial planner is just plain tacky.

Performance Reviews: The best advice when either giving or getting a performance review is to digest the information, think about it overnight and then take action. There are crappy managers out there who give bad reviews because it is within their power. Conversely, there are people who don't take criticism well. The best way to handle a performance review is to make sure you put a lot of thought into the review and are open to talking with the person about the process, their feedback and your growth trajectory.

The Entry: You know the guy who just barges into your office or cube with news, gossip or a question? Five times a day? Don't be that guy. Make sure you check to see if someone is on the phone or otherwise engaged and then ask if they have a minute to chat. Otherwise, people will start to avoid you. Really.

Computer Snooping: Never, ever, ever look at the content on someone else's computer, unless they show it to you. Even if it is right behind their head and you are being drawn to it like a moth to light. And especially don't look at their computer when they aren't there. "I was just checking something" or "My own computer went down" doesn't cut it. It is snooping and it violates that person's privacy.

Taboo Topics: If you are the best of friends with everyone at your office, that's great. You get the gold star for team player. But just because you consider all of these folks to be your "friends" does not give you carte blanche to discuss your one-night stand or your bitter break-up with them in painful detail. Unless you are truly comfortable with and truly friends with someone, don't put them into this horrible position.

What's Your Agenda? It may not be apparent at first, but everyone has an agenda in the office. Some people fly under the radar because they are doing just enough work to get by and don't want to rock the boat. Others have already designed the business cards for the VP job they are lusting after. Whatever the case, make sure you have your own agenda and don't get bogged down in someone else's mess. Align yourself with the right folks for the right reasons and don't get mired in office politics. You get farther with hard work and honesty than with conniving and lying. Except on TV. And in the movies. Okay, and in some books. But that's it.

Out to Lunch: Some people take lunch every day, while others prefer to eat at their desks or skip lunch so they can get out of work on time. Whatever your preference, be respectful of everyone else's plan. Don't harangue them about never going to lunch with you and don't judge the folks who have time to go to lunch if you don't. Everyone has their own timeframe and stress levels to deal with, so let them do what they need to do.

Pay It Forward: It's tempting to show off your title and exert your power. Everyone has the urge sometimes. But throwing your weight around may come back to haunt you. Remember that mail guy you embarrassed in front of everyone who is now the head of the start-up your company is pitching? Or the assistant you treated like crap who is now a best-selling author you want to represent? What goes around comes around. Karma-wise, be nice to everyone.

Make a Difference: It may not cross your mind to do nice things once in a while, so write it down. People remember kindness just as much as they remember meanness. It makes everyone's day when someone orders ice cream for the whole office to celebrate a big win or when everyone is allowed to leave at 1 p.m. since it is a sunny day. It's not something to do all the time, but whatever thing is within your power to spread cheer, do it.

Smarty-Pants: It is often said that money makes the world go 'round, but it's really the amazing array of people in the world. Our differences are what make us unique as individuals and as assets to the companies we work for. Believing or acting as if you are smarter than everyone else is just going to make people hate you. Even though you may have an MBA and your IQ is off the charts, that doesn't make you superior.

Invitations: When you work in an office you get invited to lots of stuff—openings, parties, meetings, seminars, classes, etc. Always graciously acknowledge the invitation and then decide if accepting is going to benefit you or the other person. Many folks make the mistake of either trying to go to everything or responding to nothing. Either way, you are the one who loses out.

The Service Staff: The people who keep the office running are many times the ones who get the least credit. The folks who clean the bathrooms, order the copy paper, change the light bulbs and vacuum the floors are the ones who keep the machine going so everyone else can get their job done with the least distractions. Remember to take a few minutes to say hello, see how they are doing and, oh yeah, thank them for doing their job. It will be appreciated and remembered.

Newbies: The first day on the job is very similar to the first day at school: You want to make the best impression while feeling like you want to throw up. It is daunting, intimidating and overwhelming to start a new job, even for the most confident of folks. Be the one who stops by to see if they need help or just to say hello. You don't have to be their best friend or help them forever after, but just help them until they find their way. It takes only a few minutes out of your day and it will mean a lot to that person. Okay?

The Mean Girls: It is natural that people tend to form cliques in office environments, whether it is within your group, with former college colleagues or with folks from the company softball team. It is positive to be part of a group and it validates us as human beings, but don't turn into the raging bitch posse that causes people to have high school flashbacks. Everyone hated those people and still imagines revenge scenarios.

Competitive Nature: A little healthy competition never hurt anybody and is good incentive to get the creative juices flowing. That said, there is no reason to take it to the World Championship level and become a mini-dictator who must have the trophy. No one will want to play in your sandbox. Ever.

Teamwork: When you think about working with your colleagues to achieve a common goal, you are either the person who is groaning inwardly or the one jumping for joy. There is no middle ground here, but there are ways to compromise. If you are a loner, offer to take a portion of the project you can do on your own and then report back to the group. If you are a natural born leader, then take on that role and project manage. You are all aiming for a common goal and group success, so play to your strengths.

Colleagues can make or break a job, so it's a great investment to make friends and be a team player. It does get to be a bit much, though, when you always have to give them money or stuff ...

Chapter Fifteen: The Money Pit

Birthdays. Check. Going-away parties. Check. Baby showers. Check. Mama needs a new pair of shoes. What? There are always things going on at work that require money and a card. You can't ignore all of them or contribute to all of them, so take your time, be strategic and come up with a game plan that works for you while greasing the right wheels.

Birthdays: The best way to handle the birthday situation is to write a thoughtful note to the person celebrating that is personal and heartfelt. You do not need to be guilted into giving cash for an extravagant gift. Most people don't even remember who chipped in for the gift, but they do remember who acknowledged their day.

Showers: Baby and wedding showers are very personal events. If you aren't close to the person who is being honored, it is best to just stop by at some point and congratulate them on their good fortune. Since they will probably have several showers, with the work one being the most impersonal, pitch in for the gift only if you really want to and if it means something to you.

Going Away: Leaving a company is always bittersweet since you have spent a helluva lot of time there over the past however many years. So when there is a going-away bash in the conference room, you should go and wish the person all the best. If it is at an expensive steakhouse and it is BYOC, then it is totally fine to take a pass unless the person is your BFF at work. Stop by and say "best of luck" and then get back to work or play.

Sick Leave: For some reason it becomes everyone's business when a coworker is out on sick leave. Maybe it's because the person's work is being done by others or because people are being nosy, but it's really nobody's business what's up with your hernia operation. Keep your few friends in the loop and ask them to respect your privacy. The only time it is appropriate for everyone to get involved in your business is when your office announces that folks can donate their sick leave to you so you can be out for longer. Otherwise, mind your beeswax.

Secret Santas/Bunnies/Hanukkah Bushes: The assumption that everyone celebrates Christmas or Easter has become more prevalent as these two holidays in particular have taken on monumental importance in the consumer marketplace. Regardless of the religious leanings of the company owners or your own personal proclivities, it is unfair for any company to assume all employees will participate in or donate money to a religiously significant holiday in the workplace. Unless you are the Christmas tree sweater–wearing kind, politely opt out of the holiday love-in.

Holidays: Most companies give employees at least five or six standard holidays in addition to their vacation time. For example, some folks get Columbus Day off and others get Martin Luther King Jr. Day. Regardless of your day, do not be pressured into paying for a lunch or some other celebration to honor that day if you are required to be at work. For example, you do not need to pitch in money for a veteran's charity on Veterans' Day. It's not necessary and not acceptable at work.

Weddings: It is customary for people to invite their closest coworkers and their boss to their wedding. The most appropriate course of action is to invite those coworkers with whom you socialize outside of work. The others may grouse for a bit, but they are just blowing smoke. They will see the pictures and ooh and aah with sighs of relief that they didn't have to go or fork over $100 for a gift.

Jerry's Kids: Is there a season of the year that is not cornered by pimping kids out to raise money for their schools? Chocolate, gift wrap, Girl Scout cookies—it's never ending. And it's a sad state of affairs for the country that a majority of the kids shucking for cash are attending public schools, but that's another story. If you like the stuff, you should buy it. If you don't, then just tell the seller that you are contributing to your own kids, your nieces or nephews, or that you are on a diet. All are perfectly acceptable responses.

Cashola: If you are asked directly for a generic cash donation by the boss or the company mascot, the best and most honest answer is, "That is not in my budget this month." Don't apologize, make excuses, feel bad or further flagellate yourself. You work there; you don't have to subsidize company-endorsed events as well.

Biz Gifts: With ethics laws as they are and the expense of quality gifts increasing every year, it is hard to know what is appropriate to accept or to give. The ideal scenario involves a token item that says something about your or their business that is useful, but not extravagant and not gross. If you work for a creative company, be creative and give a gift that the recipient can actually use and that will make them think of you every time they use it.

Tchotchkes: Depending on what business you are in, you may or may not get tons of crap in the form of T-shirts, key chains, cup holders and the like throughout the course of the year. Some people value this stuff like gold and showcase it all over their cube. Other folks couldn't care less and leave it out on the communal table with a "free" sign on it.

Awards: It is really, really nice to receive an award. Think of all the things you have won in your life and how good that made you feel. Many companies try to replicate that feeling with some sort of awards ceremony at the end of a quarter or at the end of a sales period. Even if you think it is corny or uncool, get into the spirit of the thing and bask in the recognition.

The Dreaded Raffle: There are many good things to be said for the raffle. It creates a sense of excitement and there is gambling involved—all good. However, the person running the raffle is usually chosen for the job since they have the tenacity of a pit bull. They will hunt you down like a dog and make you fork over your cash for a few tickets if it is the last act they perform on this earth. Unfortunately, this is a no-win situation. You have to buy at least one ticket or spend your days skulking around the office hiding from the raffle lady.

The Man Fund: CEOs are an interesting bunch. They make more money than all of their employees and they are privy to everyone's salaries, but these are the same folks who may encourage you to support their personal charities. You can either be a suck-up and make a donation, being sure to let the CEO know, or you can let the CEO know that you have your own charity and donate your time and money every week. Your call on the direction you take, but you do have options.

Political: Unless you work for a lobbyist, a member of Congress or the president of the United States, political fundraising is off limits at work. It is against the law and also highly offensive to many people. The workplace is supposed to be free of religious and political bias and that works in your favor. Don't ask, don't tell. But on your own time, volunteer for your favorite candidate and pass out stickers to your friends for their laptops.

It feels good to help people out, but you have to draw the line somewhere or you will be broke and exhausted. This also applies to the giving of your free time and energy for work.

Chapter Sixteen: Off-Sites

Getting out of the office for work is always a good way to mix it up a bit. The off-site or business trip is marketed to employees as a perk or a way to bond away from the office. Clasping hands for the free-fall of trust and hurtling through the air in an aluminum tube to a Midwestern destination are team and character builders.

On Board: When traveling with others for business, there are plenty of awkward moments. Planes are at the top of the list. Since you are sitting right next to someone you know, you have to talk to them throughout the flight and you also run the risk of falling asleep and drooling. The best route to take for flying with biz colleagues is to bring work to do in-flight, not to take any heavy-duty medications or alcohol before or during the flight, and to mind your own business as much as possible. Sucks for you if you have to sit with chatty Cathy from finance or sweaty Mike from marketing.

Hotel Rooms: With many companies economizing these days, it has become pretty common for staff to share hotel rooms on the company's dime. If this is the policy at your company, you may want to come up with an excuse in advance, because that is too close and personal for work. Ask the boss or HR if there are any work-arounds to the bunking system and see what they say.

Tipping: It can be very confusing knowing what to tip when you are traveling for business, especially if your company is hosting an event at a hotel and you aren't sure what is included. The best rule of thumb is to tip 15–20% of the total for services rendered, then add those tips to your expense report. Better to drop a fiver on the valet than to have your car take forever when you are late for a meeting.

The Company Card: Having a company credit card makes life easier for everyone. You, accounting, your boss. You can charge work expenses all in one place and then when the bill comes, you can submit it for payment with your backup and receipts. See? Simple. When you use your personal card for travel, everything gets mixed up. You have to expense all of your receipts and you end up missing things here and there, which invariably adds up. Always ask for a company card. The worst thing they will say is no, in which case it is then up to you to secure a personal card that you use just for business charges so you don't end up losing out.

Retreats: Retreats are a way for teams to bond outside of the office. If your company is pretty hip and happening and wants to do a retreat, make suggestions about what you think would work for that particular group. Hiking or rowing may be great for some groups, but of absolutely no interest to others, so put your two cents in and make a recommendation. Since it is mandatory and during work hours, it may as well be fun!

Bonding: People start to relax when they are away from the office and out from behind a desk. Take advantage of this phenomenon by learning more about the people you work with, talking to them about things other than work and sharing some stories about yourself. That guy you thought was a jerk may turn out to be a nice guy when the pressure is off. Corny, but true.

Drinking: Depending on the company, drinking at off-sites is either greatly encouraged or heavily frowned upon. Either way, it is best to play it safe and keep the boozing to a minimum until you either find the cool people to hang out with away from the prying eyes of management or just decide to abstain. Having drinks with the boss is only fun if they are having fun too!

Sports: For some reason it's really common for many companies to field softball, baseball, football or even kickball teams. While team sports are a great way to get in shape and let off some steam, remember that not everyone wants to or has to participate. Those folks who aren't athletically inclined and bring down the team average don't enjoy getting the stink eye from the team captain (formerly the star player at his alma mater). If you aren't down with the physical activity, get ahead of the game and offer to be in charge of equipment, lug the cooler or simply be a cheerleader. You can also just opt out.

Costumes: Dressing up and role-playing may be a turn-on for a lot of folks. Being forced to dress up for an event or to perform in a get-up not of one's choosing is no fun at all. Some companies have themed days, really get into Halloween or have variety shows as free entertainment for the rest of the staff. They are mandatory and it is frowned upon if you don't participate. As a fully grown human being who works to make money and not to provide free entertainment, it is within your rights to abstain. However, there may a very high price to pay for not joining in the reindeer games.

Playing games and breaking the rules are okay sometimes, but they aren't the strategies that are going to move your career forward. Be a team player, express your individuality and creativity, and make your presence known (even when you think it's corny).

Was It Worth It?

Maybe you think this is all a bunch of BS and you are going to do your own thing. That's cool too. Those who need these tips will take them and those who don't won't.

The most important thing to remember about business is to read the room: the people, the environment and the vibe. Taking the time to figure out what is going on, how people are responding to you and if your message is actually being received are the keys to business success.

It's hard to believe, but a lot of stuff you learn at work can be translated into life. Like how to politely talk on the phone, go out to dinner or pitch yourself. When you think about it, these all apply to relationships as well. If you get it together at work and learn the ins and outs of business, that success and confidence will spill over into your personal life. And vice versa.

If you pay attention, listen to what is going on around you, take direction and advice, manage your time and others' time wisely, and exercise respect, you will make it big. Be a good corporate citizen, balance work and life, learn from others and use your talents for good, not evil.

Not to be too Obi-Wan Kenobi about it, but you guys are the future of business. And there are a lot of you, so we expect to see great things over the next 50 years. No pressure, though.

Go forth and engage responsibly.

Bronagh Hanley is a San Francisco–based freelance publicist and entertainment junkie. In her twenty years as a publicist, Hanley has driven around the country in an RV with Roy Rogers singing songs, walked the red carpet with impresario John Waters, shielded Matthew McConaughey from gaggles of women at a Hollywood premiere, hosted a screening at The Shining hotel, seen Garth Brooks in his skivvies and witnessed the opening of the Medici family crypt in Florence with Morley Safer. Her personal life has been just as interesting, with her family arriving in the U.S. from Northern Ireland in the late '70s; growing up on Capitol Hill in Washington, DC; performing at the Kennedy Center as part of the Children's Youth Orchestra; attending the White House Christmas party five years running; inventing the Microwave Buddy (which no one ever bought); testifying before Congress; and surviving a flash flood in the Dominican Republic. Hanley is very happily married to a great guy and has an awesome and sassy little girl. *OMG! My First Real Job* is her first published book.